salmonpoetry

Publishing Irish & International

Poetry Since 1981

MW01026203

At the Kinnegad Home
for the Bewildered

JEFFREY LEVINE

Published in 2019 by
Salmon Poetry
Cliffs of Moher, County Clare, Ireland
Website: www.salmonpoetry.com
Email: info@salmonpoetry.com

ISBN 978-1-912561-38-4

Cover & Title Page Image: *Jeffrey Levine*
Cover Design & Typesetting: *Siobhán Hutson*

Printed in Ireland by Sprint Print

*Salmon Poetry gratefully acknowledges the support of
The Arts Council / An Chomhairle Ealaíon*

Contents

PART II

Ilya Kaminsky
On Jeffrey Levine's Poetry

"The best work," Paul Valery told us, "is that which keeps its secret longest."

What is our secret, our mystery?

What is clarity?

How do we see ourselves, our human moment, our planet?

*

Why are these questions relevant for poets today?

The problem for typical practicing poets today is that so many of their colleagues, also practicing poets, happen to be college professors. Why is that a problem? Because the person who is employed as a teacher needs to explain things to others all day long. This activity of constant explaining of one's own art creates a kind of loss of mystery in art. Today we have many skillful poets who teach, and also many playful poets, poet of protest, of erotics. They all also teach. Poets of mystery are disappearing—not because of science, technology, societal changes—but because the person whose daily job is to explain, explain, explain—forgets to shut up and listen to the world. Shutting up is a good way of getting one fired; one gotta keep talking. And where, one wants to ask, among our beloved contemporaries, is mystery? These days, such questions are not polite ones to ask.

Perhaps it is time for our poets to go back to the inner existence, to that dwelling space of imagination, perhaps it is time for us to ask what, in our writing, keeps the secret longest.

*

It is exactly from this perspective that I feel Jeffrey Levine's work poses a particular interest.

As any real poet, Levine understands that the spiritual seeker's medium is language. The tension of language is what makes or breaks the poem. Knowing this, the book announces, from the start, Levine's interest in clashing the language against itself to make us ask: isn't there poetry beyond language?

As the pages turn, one constantly marvels at the relationship between the physical body and the sound/meaning of words. For this poet, there is much erotic life in the very sounds of words:

> "The last word I lost was opera, he tells…and face like a spoon, opera, the music in a kiss, who abandons who, he wonders now, his mouth upon her lips."

And:

> "Meanwhile, everything living will wait….Meanwhile, she offers you wine, you don't say no. Meanwhile, you beg her to sing, and miasmas of her song are long and words are biting—"

*

Levine starts the book with a quote from Sherwin Bitsui: "The place between languages is something else."

It is an apt beginning, as it makes one ask two questions: What is "the place between languages"? And, indeed, is that "something else"?

The answer to the first question can be found in constant shifting of perspectives through the book, in the cinematic approach, in the relentless drive to bring into poetry the struggles and pursuits of great painters and composers, Levine is constantly between Rembrandt and Rembrandt, between Caravaggio and Caravaggio, between Roberts and Roberts, between himself and himself: I move the camera and your life comes out of you in colors, / I move it again, it goes back in. He is obsessed with how music and image enter our bodies. How we get to keep the language inside us, how it gets to keep us inside, too. Levine is also interested in how the langauge refuses us: It was music in an earlier life I could not take into my mouth when I was dying.

This space between languages, between mediums, between breaths, is the work of poetry. It is also the heart of mystery. After all, while the word lily in German is maiglöckchen. But in Rumanian maiglöckchen means a tear. And, then, in Russian lily is landysh. But in Kyrgiz, landysh is noise. In English we say when a star falls one must make a wish. In Rumanian language it means that someone, in that moment, has died. Words are voyages, Donne wrote, such sinews in thy milke, and such things in thy words. And, Emerson: words used to be animals.

What sets Levine apart is this: while Levine is keenly aware of the above, he is also interested in our second question: what is something else? What and who is this other? How can one reach this something else, this other, via language.

In other words: where is the mystery to be found?

The mysterious, the unseen, in almost-seen populates most pages of this book. Sometimes, it takes the shape of light:

"light, white breath of horses"

And:

"a house filled with forgotten thoughts… / in which I become / a lost thought boxed within a certain light"

And:

"No light I know as light, but winter sky on ice stealing the sky's milky hue," Levine says. "Wait, the day stops. Wait a bit more, and the day starts again."

What is this desire to see a time stop, then start again? How to capture this light in which time stops?

And, more importantly: how can poems do that? By what means of craft?

Levine is at his most revealing when the mystery is conveyed via evocative, unexpected imagery, When the moment opens with "with ice-cold spoon / snap the world open to the pulp."

It is not always this violent, of course, not always the snapping to the pulp. At times, the knowledge arrives as something almost shy—it is shy like a deer watching us pass in our cars from its trail. It sees how "stories unwrap a planet gone too long quiet and cold." It suggest how we might want to watch our own hours:

Tomorrow, we write something, each, and paste
The word *green* into it
And maybe *pear.* Yes?

Don't be sad.
Everyday, things turn

...As Emerson said on Pedantipo,
"A beauty not explicable is dearer
than beauty which..."

See how fearlessly I quote.
see, we little horses how one day ends,
it ends.

With this humility, comes mystery. Comes the ability to overhear that which is between languages:

"I hear crying. I hear it in Geez, in Urdu, in Farsi, in Japanese.
But no. Not you. Not yet. This night nothing but but bullfrogs."

Between grief and tenderness, very interesting things take place, indeed:

Sure I am filled
with grieving powers,
...it is only tenderness
that makes me put off exercising them, a woman waiting
for the precise timing,
to peel an apple
a knife peeling around a man's heart."

This, perhaps, is the key to Jeffrey Levine's poetics. This precise balance between grieving voice and tender one. This is his tonality as a seeker.

But what is his goal? What is it that he seeks? Does he want to see "how we enter into the warm breast of the future"? To watch how "we remember in advance how we will remember today"?

Perhaps. But as with any spiritual seeker, in order to stay sane, one needs a good sense of humor and a big heart. Without it, one is lost in that awful terrain of self-regard. Levine realizes this, and there is much marvelous humor here, in these pages, towards anything, from self, to others, to language ("Aramaic has been my umbrella," he says.) His humor is subtle, intelligent ("It is only hell that falls prey to memory. / On the other hand, hoping is exaggeration, / I am for exaggeration"). Over and over, one can't help but admire the wonderfully light irony with which the speaker addresses himself ("My fried Frank says, "The Fact that you move so beautifully / more or less takes care of Futurism." The world around me is terribly clean / .")

There is also much desire for others (I could not lock myself / in the bathhouse and write a symphony, he tells us). And, above all, there is marvelous love poetry in this book. "I watched myself watching her," the poet tells us. "There is so much to celebrate. She invites moments of unaccountable happiness." Nothing, no visions, no spiritual journey, is more important than the beloved in this book:

> "Just to see her soften is worth the risk of offending
> the deep thinkers"

and:

> "She can do anything she wants with him. Her flattery is nothing
> because he is already convinced."

And:

> Meet me there, in our garden
> with you, being yourself, and me,
> your own.

From this commitment, a new kind of idea of music comes in:

> "So I told her about that dream we dream
> the music in"

This is marvelous, indeed. As is this:

> "Love, he tells her, is a miracle the flesh tries to duplicate. He
> offers up his own strangeness. They are building each other a
> shelter in the larger space of their bodies"

The beloved here is that other. From this address to the other the real, beautiful, full lyric voice comes forth:

> "You pray at the bottom of the stairs.
> Shouts and cities galloping past.
> There will be a small courtyard.
> Plenty in plenty.
> An unlit street.
> Stairs sprout astonished steps."

Not everything, of course, here is love poetry. Far from that. And, yet, even that gorgeous (and also terrifying!) visionary poem, "Stealing the Fundamental Tongs," gives us not the singularity of an "I" but the larger, more communal, vision of "we" —

"We play the defenseless child, but in truth / we are the demon."

And:

We forget everything. // We forget that we are the subject of mysteries.

This opens up another interesting aspect of Jeffrey Levine's poetics: in this book the secret, the visionary language, is far more likely to be found not in the poet's address towards his innerscape, not in the obsession with personal pronoun, but in his address towards other humans. This is a unique thing, this spiritual drive that is always at its most apparent when it comes in relation to others, in tenderness towards others. As in these beautiful lines that announce both cosmic, yes, but also a very human connection:

A thousand and one sea gulls poised
on a shoal of white sand between the earth
and the watery parts of the world, which is why
Rabbi Joshua ben Karha says, "You know
that your son is mortal?"

*

Contemporary American poetry is not very concerned with such a blend of cosmic/domestic questions. That is too bad. "The best work," Paul Valery kept telling us, "is that which keeps its secret longest." Here, the secret is both intimate, and wide open. The secret is to seek the others, while joining the emotive and imaginative realm.

What is clarity? Perhaps it is the only mystery we have.

What we have not had to decipher, to elucidate by our own efforts, what was clear before we looked at it, is not ours. From ourselves comes only that which we drag forth from the obscurity which lies within us . . .

PROUST, *Time Regained*

And all faces are turned into paleness; Wherefore are your faces so sad.

GEN. 40:7

PART I

This place between languages is something else.

SHERWIN BITSUI

[Figure 1, Leporello Considers the Heavens]

Considers the wife of a poet, Austrian, with shallow breasts, a delicate inward-curving face like a spoon, lit with a sallow glow—a spoonful of clear soup—a long fine nose, a small red mouth, he sees her at once as she enters the courtyard of the inn. The last word I lost was *opera*, he tells the poet's tall and slender wife with the shallow breasts and face like a spoon, *opera*, the music in a kiss, who abandons who, he wonders now, his mouth upon her lips.

The whole thing is a hoax, said my late master, my one true master, Don Giovanni. This room. Candle. The past. It all lights up.

The Don stands under the awning that runs along one side of the courtyard. He leans into the hugely fat wife of the landlord, a colossal woman, her haunches swaying as if each one held a small girl. Never appear to doubt yourself, my master told me once—if you do—you've lost.

There is something else: the music I was caught within as if magnificent creatures were undressing, removing their wings. It was music in an earlier life I could not take into my mouth when I was dying. I was calmed the way a single note would be, brushed with a husky voice—take care of this voiceless light, lest we depart into worlds that have nothing to do with those we love.

What I meant to say, my master bequeathed to me an old book on the poisons of madness, a map of forest monasteries, a chronicle brought across the sea in Sanskrit slokas. *I hold all these within his arias*, he tells the poet's wife with the large red mouth and the long fine nose, his hand sketching notes in her Andalusian hair.

I hold his voice the way astronomers in the markets of wisdom draw constellations for each other calculating the movement of the great stars saying these, as he shows his latest where, precisely, heaven and where, exactly, hell.

Although Madame Did It on the Grill

Raking coals, straddled amid licks of flame, sparks rose up
from the earth, arced across the sky turning overhead in bright pinwheels,
as if to say, guess what it is,
>   and it was into this dream of pinwheels and sparks
>   of earth that she lay down the eggplant, the onions and
>   tomatoes, and our mouths filled with the char of it, that char,
>   and the air with the waterfall sounds of the lute, sky shapes,
>   the crisp skin a bloom of phosphors,
>   the grilled meat a dream of Frescobaldi.

Meanwhile, everything living will wait – Assisi, the high Gothic cathedral at
Rheims, Bosch's *Garden of Delights*, Newton's rooms at Cambridge. Meanwhile,
she offers you wine, you don't say no. Meanwhile, you beg her to sing, and
the melismas of her song are long and the words are biting—
>   she feeds you strips of roasted eggplant with fingers like snow and
the sky threatens sparks and more snow under that sky of sparks and snow
she adopts the tone of one who explains the obvious to a child
>   and all that night, throughout the world, a terrible noise of sheep
bleating and of bells from the church towers, of wooden houses cracking,
and the cries of men and the cries of women, and a great stream hurtles
down the mountain steps, and she takes a mouthful of air, and with the
fullness of her breath sings so low and soft we know
>   there is something more.

Licking the Bowl

After Sacrifice of Isaac, *Caravaggio*

Odd, his vulture rummaging through the chattels of the dead.
What form is there besides this one?

Vulture meat, meat of the dead, their things.
The exposures of the past, the windfalls of the present.
Neither the hoopoe nor the bat, says Leviticus.

The true paradise, perhaps: being given the keys of the house, empty,
everything gone but for a box of recipes on index cards:
My chocolate brownies.
My coleslaw with caraway seeds.
My secret recipe for apple sauce.

She was what, poaching an entire salmon for company at 8, the cake already
out of the oven, the wine breathing, when he summoned me outside for
sacrifice, as ordained.

Today, you know what, you're Isaac, ok, and God told me to get my knife
and sharpen it. Take a look at the Caravaggio in the Galleria deli Uffizi in
Firenzi. You get the idea.

Dad, you speak Italian? You know Florence?
Firenzi, he says.
Firenzi, yes. ok.
Who told you to sharpen up the kitchen knives?

You know who. But, Dad, it's only a test. God calls it off, it never happens.

Oh boy, you have a lot to learn.

O, do Thou regard the ashes of Father Isaac
heaped up on top of the altar, and deal with Thy children
in accordance with the Mercy Attribute.

In other words, I slay you. You, the lamb for my burnt offerings. You can't
show God you fear him if you don't go through with it. Otherwise it's just
practice. Otherwise, how can it matter whether the knife is sharp?

We're splitting hairs, Dad.
Look at the Caravaggio, does it look like I want to be stopped? Caravaggio got it.
Let's go, Jeff, we have some astral delirium to unleash in the air,
a calm and shining malady.

Dad, the painter is everywhere and nowhere at once, yes?
Forms and abstract contours subverted by a rippling levitation,
all trenchant powers diverted from the path.
Life grows by undulation, like a beacon without fire.
Besides, the poached salmon, the cake?
You'll miss the party, too.

Maybe, Son, but it's your name that's sinking to the ocean's floor
like ballast, to be used no more.
What is the imagination's job but to blur one life into the next?

He was talking like this, one hand grasping my throat,
a sharp knife in the other, and he says "Oooh," softly,
just a quiet "oooh"
and then gone.

God took him instead, maybe just a matter of timing.

I got up off the rock, rubbed the red bruise of my throat.
The butchers put away their white paper, the kind
they wrap their chops in, the kind that clung to my skin,
and the night nurse in her flock of pink lambs
conducting her meticulous rounds passes your door,
your empty room, your empty bed, and moves on, her hand
only a hand in the imagination where it extends a pen
and makes a mark on the chart by your door, whose presence
is immediate and perfect and born from its own startling absence.

He Delivers Unto Her His Blessings

There is much to celebrate. She invites moments of unaccountable happiness. They hide from the photographers. The cook invents traditional dishes, invites her into the kitchen and whispers the legends of his origins while, for luck, he traces her own history from lips to waist with his good hand, her profile shuddering under his measure. The guests prepare for after-dinner struggles with lubricious budding beaus. The entire nation awaits the birth of the beauty, the exotic, the blessed.

Stay, my treasure.

She can do anything she wants with him. Her flattery is nothing because he is already convinced. She is laughing with her contessa's voice; everyone admires the perfect red of her lines, sultry sway of her lines while the orchestra plays mazurkas, the men compare their stripes and ribbons. She trembles beneath her own little uniform, mismatched and tattered. There would be fanfares, antiphonal and filled with brass.

He promises her a little farm in the south with olive trees and amber light. Still, the night manager, a colonel, threatens to throw them out on the street for the indecency of their love. The colonel sees himself in bed clutching her, growing hot with the metallic clank of his medals. She lifts the colonel's palm to the offending place, but keeps the tone of her voice serious and complicitous, gives him half-smiles and adds some new detail or other each time she assures him it will not happen again.

She remembers what Kundera said about love, that it does not make itself felt in the desire for sex (a desire, he wrote, that extends to the universe of women) but in the desire for shared sleep (a desire limited to her). Kundera, after all, wrote about her niece. Her lover says that kissing her with the tip of the tongue feels like ice cream melting. Her lover says that she has taught certain sounds having a soul. Her lover says that their touching comprises the place where all their countless sounds merge into a soul.

She has brought along five changes of clothes, and with each change she is more herself. Love, he tells her, is a miracle the flesh tries to duplicate. He offers up his own strangeness. They are building each other a shelter in the larger spaces of their bodies, where they step out of time.

He blesses her. The air smells of damp earth, of spilled chocolate, and from time to time, she recognizes some land brought back by gusts of wind. With faith she delves into the customs of the world stirring below and when she feels hungry, she eats. And why not? It is all her doing, and he blesses her again.

Working with the Lepers

The Chinese believe that vinegar is envy, but they don't know everything. For example in my yard, you are not, neither are you in my crab apple tree, which I also own and so, also, the raccoons that live in the black oak across from where last winter the fence was crushed by that enormous stag who stood off-center for as long as he liked, pawing the snow for as long as he liked, until the snow turned to mud and the mud begat daffodils, which he ate until love turned into water and the water into wine and the wine— knowing all the salt spots, the swept sphere—how I will miss you there among the lepers, earning your sainthood daily, fevered and fervent, as if suspecting some ebbing sigh. See the papaya tree, its heavy fruit hinting at the visible? Pluck this world from our vision of love. Bless the wounds. Pour out the vinegar.

Lucretia, Just After

In conversation with Rembrandt

He bequeaths a certain immodesty, remakes me
of earth, pigments thick with my dusts, he
fills up the dark, earthy red of time, the cry
of music counts on my own wings, and I unsheathe,
crumpled, two leaves of papers, music of
madness, his defiance, and the light left to me, mine.

I take flight, I land in the middle of a tongue,
inside a tongue we cannot die, here
the wind always blows, no work is motionless,
the limit is not a limit, what I cannot have in one tongue
I have in another, from one tongue to the other, I leap,
and on a river bank or a slow barge our trumpets bloom.

Story of escape and navigation, of following
with our eyes the text the sky,
the martagon lily raising its head
above the anemones, fireflies dancing
in the valley and the painter's chariot recedes
where the carriage bolts into the sky, watched, all

eyes without distinguishing anything but a single flame, as
in the same way the tongues crack open their doors
of flesh and reveal their treasure, their singular music,
and there, a world inside a world inside a world,
at the same time above and below, and each brushstroke
a door, in other words, a traveler, in other words,

you have sinned, such as it was, you seem without life,
you are born a second time, embraced by self-pity,
emboldened by wine, wholly forgetful
that it must be three in the morning when I beg the chemist
for another hour's worth of pigment—for him, too late for me,
be deft, I tell him, of which survival is born.

Another mind touches the light, not here,
but where they do such things.

On Finding to His Amazement a Tuscan Red

At the time he did not recognize the symptoms and so he thought he was doing well. It turns out, he had all of them: bitter tongue (the burn of red peppers), ache in his palm, uncontrollable swelling of chaos in the frontal lobe, ache in his other palm, air tasting of salt, salt tasting of snow, like the triumph of the Expressionists, say a winter with crows. At the café, he walked toward her and spoke her name.

Unfair you will say.

Who is this "her"? Let's make it Soho, a place with white tablecloths, bowl of olives, a Tuscan red—or having left, from forgetfulness, the bill unpaid, the tablecloth stained Tuscan red where he could not help willing the other to appear. He had been thinking only a moment before of the possibility.

Unfair, you will say, who is this "other"?

As always, the artist fails because no unity is found between figures and ground, or the figure refuses the painting or the moment lasts too long or the language of his brush cannot accommodate the subject.

Other reasons: the call of the late goose in the falling snow, the call of the blowing snow, the moonlight turns moonlight into snow, and like Po Chui-i one must make a career of water and bamboo and blossom. Therefore, a lone traveler, you find yourself in rain among the yellow plums and the hungry bird flies into a new season. The river is, after all, immense, and who is left to defend against the beating of the drums?

The Sorrows of Our Gods

and if in the afternoon it is raining lightly—but not so much that the birds
are quiet—I am thinking nothing about being. A little mud, and the season
lets go, illuminates itself with light and with the promise of a light.

I am thinking, getting a ticket to the ordinary world is not contingent upon
solving epistemological problems. If I come back and someone asks *What
problem did you solve* I would have to say, I wasn't doing that kind of thinking.

You will protest.

It started with a vision. Printed in bold face, surmounted by cherubs, a
halo, and a dusting of stars, the most simple and ordinary of sights. A young
woman holding the hand of a small boy.

Like a balm for consolation, once you are planted in the world, chatter the
birds, the primary task is description. Doubtless, it is harder to imagine
what the daily life of a chiropractor is like than why we linger at the
wounds and sorrows of our gods. Are we to blame if your fragile bones
crack beneath our heavy, gentle paws? So many passages we cannot master.
Lucky, the gods feast on questions, disdain to answer.

If our gods could be seen we would squander our lives with staring, while
here, in front of me among the trees, even the rising mist makes a clarifying
light, lifting the curtain bottom to top, turning tree to tree, bird to bird,
bark to bark.

Half Matter [in a Material World]

—*After* Bathsheba at her Bath, *Rembrandt, 1654,*
Musée du Louvre, Paris

During the night of my foreign life
I felt tied to tulips by an illegible message.

First the soul swells the petals, folded
so as to exhale, next, an exclamation of red or yellow or

now the flower is going to redescend, the look,
there is no pause between the ascension toward birth

and the decline, the newly born followed by the flower
of the next generation, and already the breast swells,

this is the announcement. She's going to shout,
she's going to fall, she who is so shamefully adored

that sometimes I wonder if it isn't she who would be
my god. We are with each other like delirious lovers.

It is her portrait I paint, but I am flat on my belly before her
like a garden of impotence. There is not one

that doesn't grow its flowers in my earth.
In the stillest hour the need is worse than God's.

You know what I am saying, just as God drags
His prophets by the ears, by the hair, by the sleeves,

by the sex, her hands grab fistfulls of my own blood,
and in my body blazes a panic at the idea that she might let go,

gripping the ungrippable, she of the transparent fists.
I hurry, the force of time is terrible, the sea wouldn't know

how to resist the moon, I withdraw, excuse me, I murmur
in turn, I'm going to bed, I lie in turn, I make my own family

swallow the sands of lies and now on horseback, the hillside
is glossy. Already in the distance, her ample quivering

advance, over there, where the queen's cannon thunders,
scattering petals from here to Delft.

Egg of the Universe

I am not so remote as you suppose, having burned a hole in the heavens,
having charged your foil dishes, your mercury-slick saucers with runic warp
and crackle. I'd recovered from that first thump of creation, that instant the
egg of the universe sizzled into being on His upturned palm, and here, look,
I offer to resume my life among the mortals, sponging halva and phulka
from the shopkeepers, squeezing through the bazaar in my ragged tunic.

Look how far I've come, and pity me my journey. But who would erase the
folly of my flight? If fog upstages me, or windstorm or borealis, or if my
burning fails to dazzle, I'll boil off, a thimble of water in desert dunes. To
bathe in my waif-thin ribs of light is to breathe me live. Here in the newer
world I am reborn as child-light, hungry, warm, grinning at diatoms,
grazing in the grape arbors, amazed at indoor plumbing, giddy with the
pulsing of sprinklers across your cobalt lawns.

We are gregarious animals. We like to linger nights in the lee of riverbanks
or, in windy weather, light a fire of juniper twigs, sip our coffee, smoke, lie
down to sleep beside ancient quarries, our fleshless fingers sifting through
your stories, unwrapping a planet gone too long quiet and cool.

But touch. Time folds in upon time, rears up, quartered, bent-kneed,
supplicating—have some now before the rains come, the soft water—soft
as the light, white breath of horses.

A Spell

I'm wearing the Arctic sky for you, and here's a garden where Judas trees
blossom in the lanterned light. You may enter. I'm a soft-hearted man.
Bring your basket woven of panga panga wood filled with herbs and spices.
Bring your fires, amaze the toucans, charm the cockatiels. Ring.

See? I've dug two furrows. In one, you may plant all your worldly losses, in
the other, your half-eaten plum. Take my pockets stuffed with routes, my
budgets and five-year projections. You in green sari, dark emeralds around
your neck, recline there among the down pillows. Make me show my work.

You should have seen the smile you just gave me. Why did I send for you?
You should have seen that smile, Prophet. You should have seen it.

Mid-April Night with Blessing of Snow

After *Titus in a Monk Habit*. Rembrandt, 1660
Oil on canvas. Rijksmuseum, Amsterdam

For the fifth night no guests arrive,
midnight slips away, and of the wine I can make
neither a companion nor a roof beam.
A single note drifts, a chimney swift sleepless
beneath the eaves, seeing through the appearances of April.

Thirty years since I sold all my gold, so now, as you enter
this line, finding the cup that leads through the river
to the master of rivers, the keeper of archives, know
that the news is vast, more than shelf ice, more
than forbidden rice, more than a cold April wind.

Does she know that I stake my known life on her
for tonight I am given a storm with white flags in the sky,
and accompanied by pale, flashing beams,
astonishing sketches of horses' withers, I make my life
ready for her, accompanied by this storm of thirty

ringing days, by drums, live cannon, into my lost land,
and the white flags sweeping the sky one after the other,
I set out with greed, spitting fire white on black,
and an ocean crushes its groundswells onto the sky's rocks.
Trumpets of thunder, prodigy of prophetic music,

we animals carried on the backs of drums,
fling effaced flags onto the field while the dragon
disgorges its soul, the bulls bray like donkeys
and I want what this wanting wants
with a strength that surpasses me, I am sad

to be happy, I accuse myself, I forgive myself
to belong to the new world.
If I must accuse myself, it's only of committing
to dreams, as tonight I reenter the land of lost lands
in the body of lost bodies. The storm grows bold,

reaches every floor, spreads its rough hands over
the Sky's Asia, piles victory upon victory, in fever
forges its urgent roaring. I crush some stars
under my heel and milk spills out in long icy banners
to the applause of ivory trombones singing

enough of lightless days, more of Night's black wine.
Everything is made of her, even the sky.

Vox Humana

In my palm a paperweight
of blue glass blown
to shape the heavens.

Who doesn't within the ribs have a mossy castle?
But I need my own voice built of salt,
ocean winds quivering with gulls,

a low voice with high windows.
I signal my needs with three sprigs
of thyme in a vase of water which

is another way of saying, You,
love my taste,
a bird just hatched, blue,

the nectar of the diatom held under the tongue
and my hands, scabrous
as fish, blind fish striking against the rock.

[Figure 2, Lovers]

your eyes will empty of daylight
the way the cicadas suddenly, all together, fall silent.

——GIORGOS SEFERIS, *The Light*

I find it hard to believe, as if they told me that ivory comes from an animal, that the Egyptians embalmed their lovers with fishes' tears and linen *passe-partout* to take them to the hypogea on a reserved streetcar, an eminently Egyptian machine, to be newly served, though shyly.

The earth enters only so much as the artist will tolerate, and no more. For example, a low white translucent sky, so hard up against me—if I turn my head I feel it in my hair, in my ears. My lips turn blue when the sky enters. Figure then my surprise, not the sky but the sheets on my summer bed. Figure, as in to understand, as in, he didn't figure her the sort whose eyes empty of daylight—*figure*, after all, contains the earth, pattern, reference, forecast, image, and the fruit, the fig—as Bacon says, flowers have exquisite figures, figure then how the sky reconfigures the body, delight encounters body, its geography beneath the milky light, beneath the fragrant heat—it's a lie that lovers create their earth consciously out of small miseries of convalescence, remembering medicines, missing appointments, the vague horror of all one is.

Alone, in their bright kingdom, beneath their wakefulness, the lovers enter the perfect voyage, star-guided adventures recorded in fine logbooks. See for example Figure 1, a pacific space where dangers do not threaten, though their presence demands struggle, the wise eye calculating (figuring), the sudden swipe at circumstance.

The lovers walk ahead, clear, their hands grow into the landscape, stained with mossy shadows or their green pajamas, freed from formal tasks, of being nothing more than hands. Spiders, tents, microscopic silkworm eggs, the two come and go, inventing wars for their armies. They're lost in the half-light beyond the bent knees, at the *terra incognita* of their world, he at the whitish isthmus of her neck, she at the lowering clouds, they at the cicada's cease, at the onrush of dusk.

I Would Cross Three Africas fFor You

In conversation with Man in a Gold Helmet—*Rembrandt*

Gathering in the trees, shadows reach the door, the lost firebrands of Troy trick-lighting the banisters, and through graceful depths of night, a half-moon scythes some long-ago plains, under which I would be rocked by your touch, again, you dizzied by mine, aswim we two, two birds rising though dusts of incompletion. I carry your absence with me from room to room. I cross three Africas for you, I who make good on my promises, my throat heart-sized with astonishment as when, despite prayers and furtive kneeling, that boy doesn't call you for a day, the cad doesn't send for you, and on the third day the planet crumbles into a flash of mourning, the great abyss opens and the year's vaunted scaffolding vanishes before your icy body, the construction of the world is complete, yet my man has cities to build.

I was to be the angel of your resurrection, you dolt, the fanfare beloved among all trumpets. Without answer the crumbling crumbles, the only witness that I am given over, damned, by midnight I had renounced everything there, body, palace, oath, in favor of my damnable hope, my fatal hope that resides beyond the feasts, beyond the city, beyond the city's parlor, beyond the boulevards of Carthage, beyond the bridge, beyond the grandest parlor, beyond the ancient walls, past the spearheads littering the plains, over there, where roads and streets are unknown.

Here the bereavement starts. You recognize its landscape. How its roughness speaks to us. I have the greed of goats for it. It promises us thirst, solitude. It promises us enraged hope. It delivers us wholly naked, which is to say, the dusts of imperfect gods falling beneath a sky filled with clouds, and of what the sky is made: of arms, of hands, of fire.

Antiphonal

She took remnants of almost transparent yellow; lacy peach-colored teddies; slips, nubbly jackets made of the 'waste silk' spun from scraps of broken cocoons.

—GRACE DANE MAZUR, *"Silk"*

As are you spun from scraps
of distance, which own you,
while the eyes, wide with longing or desperation—

*[Thousands of feet above, an attenuated
finger of cloud pointed
across the line where the street curved away.]* // repeat

*[A cool, salty wind blew
along the street.]* // repeat

Suppose tears dropped
warm, then cool,
onto the ridge of the cheekbone.

You would wipe them with a forefinger
lest they mar the silk, and in touching
move, and in moving—

*[A battered van with corrugated tin sides
delivers silk flowers to the vendors]* // repeat

*[A woman takes crosses, statuettes
and prayer books bound
in silk from a box and sets them out on a folding table.]* // repeat

An iced bottle of mineral water appears before the peach-colored
teddies, a breath past the almost transparent,
and a glass and a bowl of pistachio nuts set down
before you by a bar hand in a silk tie.

[In the distance, in front of the courtyard,
a gardener waters the drive,
keeping down the dust.] // repeat

If you reach for the water pitcher in the distance,
the silk moves, transparent, peach, as if these overflowing
your arms—

[All of the pictures, rugs, chandeliers
and wall hangings
have vanished, while three boxes
support a thick plywood
on which are spread the remains of a lunch.]

Suppose it is not a tear that falls, but something else.

[The floor is an open plain of marble.] // repeat

[Across the square, musicians have assembled,
 arranging the music
made of waste silk spun
from scraps of broken chords upon their stands.] // repeat

Distance hangs there like an asterisk.
It wants to gather up something peach,
something transparent yellow,

as if this, overflowing.

Arabia Petra

AFTER DAVID ROBERTS,
Mosque of Omar Shewing the Site of the Temple, 1842

Night covered my small caravan where the Agha wished me to pass the
night with him, though two horses stood in place before me, steam rising
from their flanks, and beyond, the hut lay open, mere roof of branches, not
a twig in front. I reminded the Agha of an aqueduct we passed at noon,
ruined convent at the mountain base from whose top the devil showed the
way to all the kingdoms of the world. Moonlight that night as I never saw
before. All the women out of doors joined arms, circled, keeping time to
the music of their voices. With bare hands they brushed glowing coals from
braziers, their bodies bathed gold and rust as smoke of sandalwood coiled
upward into dark.

Another hut was needed for my lodging-place. A blue boat on its side
nursed the front to form a wall. Built by a Maltese sailor, carried across the
desert on a dromedary and launched on the Sea of Galilee, she molested
Arab traders until banished to stony land—now gateway to Arabia Petra,
intaglio city lain a thousand years beyond the Nile known only to the
Bedouins—convent at the mountain base from whose top the devil showed
us the way to all the remaining kingdoms of the world.

The Jewish Bride

In conversation with Rembrandt

Life of my life. Truth of my days that from afar I perceive
burning, at the stroke of midnight I am his. I give him
all if have. I kill my oxen and I distribute them,

I kiss my father and the people who are all I have
though in the end we loved more, and loved less,
than we had thought, and in the end we loved those

we had thought we didn't want to love,
and this error, this injustice, was the very way
of love, and always we were paid back and punished

not according to our merits and our mistakes
but according to grace, we were lauded for what cost us
nothing, and for what almost cost us our skin,

nothing at all, we answer for the crimes
we are accused of but not for those we are not
accused of, and sometimes what does best

for a person is her portrait, minute, tireless,
because it is not enough for us to have been born,
to be in possession of our existence, we want

to be looked at, to enjoy our brilliance, Father,
tell me I am beautiful, give me the word
that gives, sing me the legend of Me, make

the brilliance of my ordinariness beam, the mystery
of my blackness, offer me the anguish
that pierced me, the wounds, the terrors,

the assassinations, draw them on canvas
with brilliant words, I want everything,
even shame. Don't make me cross the world

without my face and without my keys, a painter.
May I have my own substance, of palms,
diamond, my sparkling love, tell me

about my fingertips, my calm lips, my bird-
likeness, paint my bride-likeness, paint me
as I am protected from falling by the balustrade

of an arm. True, we are not very beautiful,
but we are not impossible—paint us without symbol,
bathed in the soft light of what is almost ours.

Other Effects

No light I know as light, but winter sky on ice stealing the sky's milky hue. Three dim miles in each direction, to the bruised horizon to the south, the morning sluiced with white. In far fields the sun breaches in the east, wet and glowing, like a whale rolling slowly over in weightless sleep, knowing how to wait. My feet rest on a crust of snow. Chipped away, there might as well be sea ice, opaque, dark and cold, 13,000 feet to the numbed trench, like the island of Oodaaq where no one waits. This day, the sun loafs a flat path moving not across but around the sky, through it. Wait for the sun to rise in winter, wait for the moon to set. The one neither, the other nor. Wait, the day stops. Wait a bit more, and the day starts again.

Perhaps unspeakable history,
and this seepage proceeds,

as you turn the corner, find a wool carder or piano mover, maybe an art historian smeared with paint, a shepherd wearing a fleece jacket while holding a little basket filled with pyramids of cheese.

A terrible burden, knowing the possibility of joy, and so for years I have carried an arrow of flint in my pocket. Sharp and thin, it bears a birthmark, seven flames rising, like those seen from a higher place, looking down at evergreens, branches extended finger to finger, all aflame.

Like the unspent arrow, certain mornings are perfectly made.

The sun leaps up from the low horizon, trumpets its bright music. Blueberries appear in a perfectly white ceramic bowl, the coffee flows dark and darker, the flint pocketed, sheathed in fleece.

How our small planet spins inside this larger earth, our faith in the rope-makers. Leaping and taut, how the night stretches like the bow.

At the shepherd's shoulder a waterman shouts, and along the streets, still roughly laid out, doorways open or half-open where a carpenter works his plane. Or, in another variation, a smith strikes his anvil in a festival of sparks, and farther on someone takes pies from an oven that glows like a cat's mouth.

That's what happened, drop by rusty drop. Such are days of lost summers, you coming in and going out, full and pale through the rooms, your parcels filled with intrigue and chocolate, my fingers flying at the boxes, tearing like arrows at the bows, flinging them open.

The Anatomy Lesson of Dr. Nicolaes Tulp

In conversation with Rembrandt

Everything perishes under the paintbrush as stony
contemplation tears at the canvas, and he must paint
without hoping to reach what he hoped.

The soul of painting lay in the fatal desire to conquer.
He breathes rage. Disgust for wisdom,
the urgent need to seize the sky by its hair,

the gods by their feet, to unseal the sun, to drag
the whole of nature along in his triumphal procession.
At any price, to paint the forbidden,

crammed full with scented absence.
And the truth, if found: he would go so far
as to slaughter in order to contemplate

more deeply still. "The world is a chest,
and I want to paint the living heart," he said.
"And in order to paint the world's heart,

one must paint with one's own heart
equally naked," Rembrandt's horrible joy
before his canvas, his agony visible:

Silence bursting with all its might, for he was painting
with all his might, every nerve ending, bough,
rib, drawn arched stretched to breaking,

a consecration of the house of organs,
awful body vibrating under the massive weight,
and Rembrandt keeping a mad fool's silence about his madness

in a breathless hand-to-hand battle—
legs shackled, gripping himself with each brushstroke,
wrenching his arm from his arm, his chest crushed

by his chest, himself turned against himself,
painting beyond painting, bloody, skinned, his teeth
clenched upon the cry, painting his prey, painting astride

a foaming horse, pursuing an army in retreat,
and in the end racing over the body of Aris Kindt fast
becoming a famous canvas beneath his feet.

He burst out laughing, drunk with his own genius.
"I conquered Rembrandt," he told his wife,
"and I led him to victory."

"One day," he murmured at dinner, "I'll end up
painting astride my own corpse."
The studio behind the door seemed inaccessible

even to Rembrandt. A dream. No one would see
what he had painted. Not even himself.
He had a cramp in his calf.

The true Rembrandt, he could have wept from it.
At night, eyes open in the dark, lying
in his boat, he wondered who, at daybreak,

would come ashore.
Awaiting with a dead man's impotence
his resurrection.

If it ever comes about, he thought, I will paint
a self-portrait, I will paint all, I will tell all,
I will make my secret shine, I will dazzle

the whole world with horror.
And if I cannot do it directly, from the very first stroke,
then I will approach it sideways.

I'll start by painting an ox of manganese
to sell for fifty-seven oboes—and the echo
of galloping stars to listen for

when the cave wall fades into a picture,
and the picture into that trembling
the morning before the world began.

All Ten Thousand Mountains

Tomorrow, we write something, each, and paste
the word *green* into it
and maybe *pear.* Yes?

Don't be sad.
Every day, things turn
into other things.

As Emerson said on Pedantipo,
"A beauty not explicable is dearer
than a beauty which . . . "

See how fearlessly I quote.
See, we little horses how one day ends,
it ends, and another, pear green
(salvator mundi)
starts

Part II

*Then flew one of the seraphim to me, having a live
coal in his hand, which he had taken with the tongs
from off the altar. And he laid it upon my mouth, &
said, Lo, this hath touched thy lips; and thine iniquity
is taken away, and thy sin purged.*

(Is, 6, 1-7)

At the Kinnegad Home for the Bewildered

For example, when I imagine what it would be like
to be Jackson Pollock in the act of doing what he did
it feels natural to vocalize and at times to dance. Yet.

If you played a jig, reel or hornpipe in a church
when I was young you'd have been excommunicated
on the spot, or sent here, to the Kinnegad Home for the Bewildered,
say my guides, each consoling the other, as they are fairly well
Irish, as you see, though I am not, but for the odd
O'Donovan of Cork on my mother's side
and the volunteer Eamon in my middle name,
for all the difference that has made.

Or else, Pollock might have written in his Galway notebooks
had he been, ever, in Galway and written of it
rather than painting instead his maps:

Pollock himself wrote me:

I am standing atop one of the slight inclines that fall off
into the harbor—the staircase isn't steep and I can clearly see
beneath me the bustle of inner worlds, boats at the docks
and electric lamps, the density of people coming and going, gesturing . . .

and so I answered him, I can hear their shouts mixed with fiddles—
who would have thought that heaven could lie beneath?
All of these visions contrast indelibly with my limbo,
everything here is quiet, and no oysterman's cart seems to pass
on this narrow, ill-lit, unpaved road, and the angels
in the cemetery beyond fly uncanny low.

Just as fishing fleets have had their way with me, making of the maker the made,
so there is no point complaining that Pollock was himself never in Galway.

Like a grain of sugar in the shell,
like the lightning that blanches the nets,
like the line of rain-dusted ravens that seesaw
from tree-line to the livery yard beyond,
like the twilight between one me and the other,
on this terrace, every gesture suggests another voice to hear,
astonished about the boys and their horses
in the last reluctant spoiling of the day where
whatever follows any space is something new,
or so I thought, who had the brush.

All the lives that lie in front of me are gateways to other worlds.
These worlds are in no way extraordinary worlds.
Neither unimaginable, nor any less mad.

Low-Hanging Orb, Smudged Green

Press to the windowpane one warm hand,
mix the scent of skin with the taste of firelight.

With the rusted knife,
slice three gold-green apples,
wedge of cheddar,
scoop of jasmine rice.

With ice-cold spoon,
snap the world open to the pulp.

With a gesture almost gentle, snare
the ripe globe of it from the branch.

With your sharp teeth
sing a new sacrament,
fill it to the rind with juice.

A Midsummer Night's Basho

I had made my mind up.
I blew out the candle.
My head whirled in the dark with my future.
It was almost absurdly easy.
A midsummer's night.
The dark trees lashing one another,
humming the words of Basho into the wind:
I believe there is no place in this world that is not
an unreal dwelling.
Real luggage piled beside the door, the good stuff smelling
of old leather and silver clasps dating back
to the time I had thought of entering the seminary.

It would mean learning Hebrew.
It would mean plucking endlessly at the white
billowing sleeves of the rabbis.
I tell you, the rabbis in the city
are so well dressed, their shirts
of a surpassing whiteness,
having forsaken
rabbit pie, cheese and sausages, fried cod
for the purity of language.
I would learn to make declarations of love—
for the rabbis, for their wives
and mistresses, for their shirts, white.

It was not possible.
The problem with Brooklyn is a lamentable dearth
of palazzos—no views of snowy mountains from the side
window, no cloud
floating white and ocher out over the sea.
No gondoliers.
Yet there are the fiddlers and guitar players,
and fishes of lawyers
and blind men, sailors, water sellers, ice sellers, flower sellers.

The parks overflow with drummers and dogs,
with rabbis and more rabbis, and I'll tell you what.
Each one has at the very center
of his chest, a beating heart.
Hearts beating back the night in its long black coat.

I, too, come from a city of rabbis.
Aramaic has been my umbrella.
So much for the sky, but below, the deaf sea
rolls in, and a palm lifts up to catch
a miracle of fish
in a minor scale, though nobody mistakes
the heavens for kindness.

Tonight the sky is strung with upturned
palms and with lashing leaves and in the center of it all,
the sound of Hebrew.

So easy to make up the mind.
So easy to blow out the candle
hard against the hard granite outcroppings of—
you should forgive the expression—*the future*.
So easy to say.
Even a child believes in time.

Blue, and Calling

The blinds of midnight are your hands saved from freezing.
Such is the heart, and that pause, the somber hollow beneath.
Sweet prophet, I name you and your ancestors fidget.
I say your temples spill with losses
and your shadow bursts with laughing.
I say morning thickens with peregrines, flowing soft
above the waves, flowing soft with tropic history clinging
to their talons, and the skies are flayed and silent,

as when the baker slips his first bread from the oven
and beyond, street lamps wick in and out, lost in mist.
Your lover pulls a blanket to her shoulders, returns
to sleep while, a thousand years in each direction farmers
mindless of cold bring in the hay, their chickens dusted with snow.

Winter sky whitens the roofs and shutters, the shrubs
and picket fences cloaked with morning light
and pitch-black birds perch across the inert country.
Here, your bed is a leftover, day-old, frozen,
hard as amber, and as clear.

I live in your image as you live in mine, says the scripture.
So I send you a peregrine, blue, and calling.
A bird, a pond, night into morning,
the air tastes each arpeggio, note by note.

Frogs

The bad men want nothing to do with me, neither do the women, nor their sons and daughters. I am an insurance policy, mortgage, rampart, last defense. Perimeter prepared, I set out armed patrols, but my children move through my defenses like soft brie. You should hear what I hear—gunmetal groaning blue-black along the trenches as a holy incandescence lifts. You'd think it theater, a parody of fair play. Your child will want something more concrete from me. Our ephemera who art in ephemera, ephemera be thy name. That's what I hear, prophet. Is that how it sounds to you down there? Maybe I should have devised a fresh excuse before creating these creatures, pretended illness, made some better account of my principles, but in the end, one trains eons for this position, admires all his life the sculpted figure of restraint, cloaks himself in loyalty to his biographers. I promised I wouldn't forsake love, and my people laughed, one hand upon my Word, the other at their daggers' hilts, shanks gleaming and cackling like crows. Seeing me as kindly was, you will agree, contrived. Such ideas cause nothing so much as a useless kind of yearning. Do you mind a brisk hard-bitten truth? You can drink up at the Café Elysium, pose naked for Monet, tease the satyrs, but I hear crying. I hear it in Geez, in Urdu, in Farsi, in Japanese. But no. Not you. Not yet. This night nothing but bullfrogs.

[Figure 3, Imagine the body as hand]

An elusive change comes over the streets and hills,
not so much a brightening as a slight quivering
of brightening hues, as the air smites itself
with hesitations or doubts.

                       The body is a place beyond
questions, our only native land. Yet every age projects
its own image of the hand into its art.

The history confirms this proposition, and history
is row itself upon row of images, though a vision of nothing

does not come out of nowhere, as when the hand is not here,
how lovely to understand, its
                       absence is mere absence.

Sure I am filled
         with grieving powers, and it is only tenderness
that makes me put off exercising them, a woman waiting
               for the precise timing,
                       to peel an apple
a knife peeling around a man's heart.

I could, for example, drop my job, sail away on a cargo boat,
               start a new life in Iceland, in Galilee,
I could lock myself
         in the bathhouse and write a symphony.

I could pick followers, start a movement
         that shutters and sweeps like fire across the plains.

where yesterday, you see, your hands opened like apple blossoms
         when they first adore the light,
        when petals don their red devotions,
            then scatter through moonlight into mist.

At supper the child

Her eyes on the window, says, "I suppose
you were all sitting here, facing the fire
like this, before me, when I was in heaven."
It's like sleeping in a haunted house and *not* seeing the ghost,
the tide full-in, and the sea faintly gray green,
few people about; at sea the hulls of small yachts
wintering at their moorings, the fishing fleet moving out
into the gloom of the east coast, smacks painted gray
and green with their crews on deck. I envied them
their free life, their eventual sky intense, tinged
turquoise, pink-gold soft opal in the morning.
A barmaid of a morning in which masterpieces grow
like grapes on the vines that furrow Provençal farms
like foreheads, in which Dinu Lipatti gifts us
with transcendent Chopin, though he succumbed
to cancer at 33. That Tolstoy lived forever is a consolation,
or that Brahms, just long enough.

Better we should fall in love with a gypsy, not one
with fiery eyes but rather almost abstract, faint blue
or pale blue-gray, like some twilight seas meaning
almost but not quite nothing, giving nothing away,
wishing always she were somewhere else,
in another sort of life, another sort of body.
Like those Lithuanians who come together each morning
at the pier, standing far apart, without speaking
with their fat tanned faces, hat brims turned up,
as though to say, "Blessed are the meek,"
all the way around.

Riverbeds in which

small tribal children, preserved unknown
through ten centuries of human history, dodge piranhas
along an uncharted channel of the Amazon under a canopy

woven of scarlet macaws, toucans, nighthawks and the odd
blue, chocolate-making monkeys, they, all of them, lifting
their curious faces, slow grins ripple

beside the still waters, where the rocks move
even more slowly than the water,
and everywhere, like it or not,

an ebbing tide births thirteen billion
diatoms through its autumnal mouth,
washing out to sea, bending along the banks

beneath brilliant archers, their quivers emptied,
their bows pulled taught into lyres,
trained into a week of lutes,

rounded into a month of guitars,
their fingers baffled with gauze, eyes filling
with cypress and live oak.

The gesture is all Zen,
gripped hand extending outward,
thumb rigid, poised, like a stone against

the opposing stone of palm, even without arrows,
nor lamp, nor pool of light, nor mollusk,
and attached to each hyper-extended thumb

night history of pacing, a day history of waiting,
a vortex of pauses, but look: there is no enemy,
there is no Other braced by earthworks.

There is hardly a sun, and the planet, well,
we know about the water and its spawn of news,
new and old and aging in a quiver of its own.

Just so, the legions arrayed in Roman columns,
cordons, phalanxes, a river of smiles, so tall
in their Junoesque figures under sundresses and tunics,

standing marbled in their unbroken arms, wine flagons,
loaves of hot bread, each ex with stick of butter and
a better idea than forgetting the arduous world

where it's the sound of words that pierce the heart,
felling timber and sluicing water,
honing the sickles and milling the wheat.

The garden began with a large black crow, turned like the world, upside down

We were wrapped in each other's thoughts,
collecting and inhaling, immobile like the lions.
We found ourselves at the center of a passionate chastity.
The garden began. Ibises, windfall tulips, two-
thousand-year-old storks. A large black crow, which time
and weather had painted completely black,
passing by to the west of its own immobility
noticed that we were unsurprised to find it upside down,
knowing from our intimacies that we were all
of the same garden, obeying the same laws.

We each looked at the other like it is forbidden to look at someone,
with a slow, delicate surprise, dreaming, leaning over the map
of our own strangely foreign country, thinking, it is here that I live,
yes, it is here that I will dwell, dreaming the length of the lips,
contour of cheeks, musing on the missing herd of goats,
on the always hidden, always familiar rivers bathing
in the calm light of the eyes.

Far away an entire continent drifted by without bothering us.
This is how we enter into the warm breast of the future
where time spreads out at a single stretch like a field that shows
all four faces of our seasons on its furrows at the same time, our gaze
fluttering around the clock ten years from now,

we remember in advance how we will remember today past,
an immense forever pursuing itself from one today to another.
At that moment we were each the other's newborn.
The night held back its countless harbingers of anguish

and we each thought it right that for ox and lamb they had lion
and lioness. Ordinary woman. Ordinary man.

Xanthippe

A lump of plaster falls from the façade.
I have not yet by a long chalk drunk, thinking all the time,
"I am falling," and occasionally strike a rock on the way down
in case I should forget I was falling, where by falling,
I mean a clumsy, lumpish ox in a rococo salon.
Another lump of plaster gone.

As to the direct object of my free fall,
that she is on the brink of plumpness, at the moment
she is superb, the best figure among all those pointing
at the too substantial likelihood of the future.
Her eyes are not Antwerp blue, exactly, nor Nile green,
but alive, and worthy of kisses.

Philosophy gives us a kind of complex sublimation,
as another lump of plaster falls from the façade,
as if to say the experience of the lifting of a mask
is one of life's most transient, moments
which redeem the mass of time, during which
even plaster has revelatory ideas, as in:

Just to see her soften is worth the risk of offending
the deep thinkers who think me into being
at play in the treachery of words:
The death of Socrates for example, losing
an argument with her perfection.

One has to know how to change bodies.
Be first a dove then a dream then pure
means of transport, fleshless feet walking
on pebbles of air, not looking, not feeling
the serrate edges of six-month days,

not breathing, endless swimming without
olive trees and without stopping, not
going to parse the problem of Nothingness,
searching with the eyes on the thick surface
of the waters for a sign, a branch, a leaf of paper,
barely written in the coming clean of light and wind.

Am I to become profligate as if I were a blonde?
Or religious as if I were French?

—FRANK O'HARA, *Meditations in an Emergency*

With each passing hour I lose the memory of the house.
Here's how to think of this loss as something noble.
Just as we lose one day the taste of the bread of joy
and the memory of joy, so also will we one day lose
that tenacious taste of sorrow.
Even the earth forgets.
This is its strange privilege.
It's only hell that falls prey to memory.
On the other hand, hoping is exaggeration,
and I'm for exaggeration.

We wash our shirts as if we fear neither separation nor loss nor
even fading. We'll return to the huge house at the summit of Mount
Ararat and there find the future preserved.
As if there was never something to regret.
Even iron fades, swept clean, and something
magnetic sticks in my chest. A breath. A key
that won't turn. I can't open the door.

My friend Frank says, "The fact that you move so beautifully
more or less takes care of Futurism."
The world around me is terribly clean.
It looks like snow.
And the absence of the voice of God deafens me.
But on the tenth day noise returns, with untidiness, shoe
prints in the kitchen, grass breaks through the tiles
as if to say, immortality is going to sprout again,
say it with such determination, each day contested,
beset by the stuff of besetting, rescued and released,
like a thousand routed armies.

The Art of Aqueducts

So that it would not be caught within the sounds of itself,
or in the dense rain of her hair,
it would, rather, speak the art of aqueducts

saturated, house, voluptuous

with total clarity the fervid precision
of every movement, of every movement
a dream, confidential, particular.

The truck is a battered thing, corrugated tin sides.
It brings corn to markets, tomatoes, berries,
late summer flowers, dirt-caked at the roots
and wet in a copper bucket for tonight's table.

The air has clarity, a brackish,
seaside astringency,
and there in the house where we
have been sea stung and creased with salt,
the scent of coming and going.

Flowers trembling in their own music,
the way they do.

The truck grinds down the hill toward the sea,
and we are stunned by a silence made
of departure.
The gospel sings like a ram's horn.

Notes from the Book of Frailty

Call the camels back from the Tuvan steppes. Give the damn horse a name.
Watch the silver-sandaled shadow slip away, as if there were suddenly a
roof, a bed, a terrace on the sea, a table, shared—everything there wasn't
this time, this winter, a country is created inside us where we have
unknown appetites, each a sudden need, unexplained, but fruits of the same
winter, to have ten hands, or perhaps ten voices. Never had there been so
many bursts to pluck, and without explanation but only night dreads to tear
us open, and from inside we see how the first thought already sees the first
fingers of the next, and in it the premonition of the first outstretched hand,
that first contact, so slight, so cautious, this union between existing and
not, this exhausting invention of each fistful of earth, each mouthful of air
and the taste of devouring, the taste of being devoured. Yelling louder than
any god, no longer the first to sing in his language, to become the night
peacock circling a light, going mad in a forest of reflections.

Task Me, Trapeze Me

You devil who stoops to sip,
hiding your light under a bushel—
a steely thing, snatching copper
from the roofs and belfries
of the Gothic quarter.

I watched myself watching her
leave, return, return, return.
Pocketing her wake.
Reeling in her wake.

Always we are too alive to know
when it starts, but that
her breath, brushing my face,
her arms a whiff of bonfire, damp,

and dried flowers and this time
a halo of amber that seemed
to float in the air like a cobweb
trapped between mantles.
It's by the ladder that we pass
with a breath from one cloister
to another, from laughter to blush,
glimmer to our North.

Growing distant, we grow large.
It is unavoidable, this obscure
jealousy toward all travelers.

The chosen.

I leave to the reader, which is to say,
you, all responsibility for this scandal,
as if the last day were promised me,

and if then young enough, and if
halfway standing up in the boat
of the great travelers, how would I find
the breath to be born at last in a foreign land.

Meet me there, in our garden
with you, being yourself, and me,
your own.

The Inch-Wide Heart

One maintains certain standards given the vaguely wolfish shiver at the thought of the beloved, even in the presence of the beloved, though the beloved thinks, "Thank goodness it's you, not that madman who came last time, he seemed drunk to me or else lunatic." And in truth, who else to ask? You beg for a signal—god loves me, she loves me not—a whisper, a crumb of holy presence, and gods, in their infinite wisdom, and perhaps overwhelmed by the avalanche of requests from so many tormented souls, omit to answer.

He never, you notice, any more, answers.

Faith, just so, a fractious thing, and if so then, Freud is even harder, who supposes that we're all made of disobedient little lover material enshrined in our heavenly bodies. If you had to choose one or the other, the flow of blood to the brain or to the loins, we'd be better off growing fat like an actuary, plunging soft sponge cakes into our coffee.

So why shouldn't you ask? Will there be another kiss, is this or that volcano at the point of eruption, with a libido of igneous magma yet the heart of an angel?

Light the candle, conjure up that halo
of amber light, reveal the dancing shapes
upon walls that weep with tears of dampness,
the fallen ceilings, the unhinged doors,
through which, bright
moons in the courtyard
glow countless.

And What of the Redhead in the Supermarket?

So I told her about that dream we dream,
the music in it.

If the body speaks, then that's that.

And by extension, why are we asked to hear an entire song
just to pause by the overtones?

Why this lingering?

With each drop of commiseration comes
a reliable clutch of fools, the usual suspects
order the mouth's mad music.

The trick is to be delighted with the interruptions,
the bad accents, the loud ties.

In this corner: the myth of perfect beginnings,
a universal tradition—

in the other: paradise is defeated by degrees
simply because defeat is imagined.

And what if we refuse to allow the loss
the way wolves howling *no, no, no*
under a simpering moon likewise refuse?

Here in this orgy of figures
and constants we call the universe
is the repetition of the fundamental rhythm:
periodic destruction and re-creation,
the soul's best hands.

Myth is only the last stage
in the assembly of the soul—
not the abstract thing, but that trembling you feel
when you're too tired to sleep.

You call out, another wolf alone in a barren country.
The city burns with a hot, stiffish wind,
sits deep beneath the mounting sand.

I squander boxes heaped into other boxes

as they fall through a veil of snow,
see where I have made tracks for you, many toed and slow
footed in the mountains, almost catachable, nearly
benevolent
      through lights of the lanterned valley,
            wind through sparse pines,
            wind through birches,
     breath of smoke and sage, I am not pitch but arrows.

Now, for grace I look for seal and fish to feel Inuit,
            sweet scrimshaw behind ice walls and
   at 1 A.M., fashioned by Sedna, goddess of the animals of the sea,
        received by thick hands and whalebone minds, belly-filling
   as the verses translate themselves from the language of frost.

When you're too high in the world looking down
     through a mackerel sky, you cannot see
   what's precious below. You have only to rinse the rice
with cold water and cover with grasses.

Soon, there will be heat enough. A melt, a face
     at the window, a house filled with forgotten thoughts,
        a month in which I become
   a lost thought boxed within a certain light.

Whiplash Beauty, an Offering

[*Middle English* offren, *from Old English* offrian, *to present in worship.*

a. To put forward for consideration; propose; offer an opinion.

As if she had made some piping demand and refused
to be hushed, as if relieved to be free of the narrow streets
and passageways of the city fading behind, to be staring
out to sea, as if beyond the walled island, the chapel
and small stone jetty and the bluish early morning
mist a blue sun rinsed a blue boat, small and precise.

b. To present in order to meet a need or satisfy a requirement.

One worries about minimum upkeep.
Her house begins as wood and ends as wood.
You are required to know the seasons' birds
and the afterglow of the winter sun in snowy meadows.
She appears. You are no longer tired from walking.
Your rooms, suddenly bigger, you understand as if for the first time
once impenetrable philosophers—
who you are now permitted to forget.
You can mix any three oils into a miracle of color.
She will know that song.

c. To propose as payment; bid.

You are looking at a large photograph.
She lets you hold it for a few seconds.
She lets you take it in your hands.
A woman on a balcony is smoking a cigarette.
The print is grainy and indistinct,
taken from some distance and enlarged many times.
She lets you hold it for a few more seconds.
She takes it from you and returns it to the bookcase.
Perhaps we should leave.

d. To present as an act of worship: offer up prayers

You pray at the bottom of the stairs.
Shouts and cities galloping past.
There will be a small courtyard.
Plenty in plenty.
An unlit street.
Stairs sprout astonished steps.

e. To exhibit readiness or desire (to do something); volunteer: offered to carry the packages.

Which have been instructions more solid than red brick.
Which is now a palm open beneath.
Which will be dew covered if we don't hurry.

f. To put up; mount: partisans who offered strong resistance to the invaders.

The long way takes you by the seafront
A less crowded descending street.
You agree about the photograph
And what she had meant by (p)reparations.
Buoyant. Pointing out. In reply.

g. To threaten: offered to leave without them if they didn't hurry.

The sun fades by degrees through nursery blue
to diluted milk, effected, across the line
of the horizon.
As yet there is no intimation of night
in the eastern sky, and below the shop awnings,
washing hung like bunting
from wrought-iron balconies.
You unfold her offer.
What is written there.
Gilded.
Spill.

Stealing the Fundamental Tongs

Memory is useless. Even God,
who forgot until sunset of the sixth day
to fashion the first set of tongs—without which,
nothing—thus completing the work of Creation,
then forgot where he put them.
The first poem was a tool, then, and the second
loss—we forget this.
We forget everything.

We forget that we are the subjects of mysteries,
descendants of known or unknown dates, frail seeds
of memory lifted and carried up to our prenatal heads.
We forget it's the sensual, superincarnated pressure
that makes us do what we do, eyes closed, lips closed:
the oath, the alliance with ancestral desire.
We play the defenseless child, but in truth

we are the demon, the goat, the man on the pyre,
the orphan's revolt, the widow's warrior—we
have drunk, we have eaten, we have changed species.
We walk in such darkness and we never know
if we are the child, the father, the grandmother,
the dwarf, the conqueror, the hero is not what we think.

And those we love most in the world
and for whom we paid at the entrance to the path
in a single stroke our whole life, and in cash,
we cannot even say with conviction why.
Memory is useless, sight is useless.
We pay cash for the seer, who turns out
to be second-sight impaired, without rights.

We pick some flowers and the seer bounds
out of the forest, throws us to the ground,
and demolishes our engine with his ancient tongs.
He strikes our spokes, our handlebars, our fenders,
the bell, our bell, our trumpet, steals our memory,
curses our trumpet, takes our flowers, feeds them
to the live coals.

Getting It Right

You find the scudding base of familiar sky
in a saint about to fall, cool in your vows
in country sleep, mud dripping, hatching
ship-work and chucked bells, a blood-
counting clock, face of hands, but then

your own son, your very own mud-hatched
ship-work told you once when he was barely
old enough for language that the breath
draws back like a bolt through white oil and
a stranger enters like iron, or you could swear
he did, out of his own mouth,
and something rings like the beginning
of prodigies, now you could swear to it.

Hold on. It's not impossible to surprise dark matter
into glowing like a bolt though white oil, hold
these chucked bells, toll the scudding base of sky,
boundless, without a trace of wind, perfectly smooth,
the sand barely spun.

Let no one set foot here. No one else.
The translucent air of winter at noon,
and in it, the pure emptiness is full of birds.

A thousand and one sea gulls poised
on a shoal of white sand between the earth
and the watery parts of the world, which is why
Rabbi Joshua ben Karkha says, "You know
that your son is mortal?"

The noise of the air is a slight vibration inside silence.
This is the sound that allows the sea gulls to breathe
sunlight, their thousand and one white breasts turned
like yours, toward the light.

This ceremony takes place in the absence of witness,
in furtive contemplation, this man unauthorized
to attend this mystery. Look—

the gulls sense the slightest glance—and all is scattered.
Like the one where the boy says,
I move the camera and your life comes out of you in colors,
I move it again, it goes back in.

Acknowledgments

I wish to thank the following magazines and journals where many of these poems first appeared, often in different forms, some so much altered as to be nearly unrecognizable, for which I apologize to those many gracious editors at: *Agni, American Letters & Commentary, American Literary Review, American Poetry Journal, Barrow Street, Denver Quarterly, Diner, Ekphrasis, Fugue, Harvard Review, The National Poetry Review, New Orleans Review, Ploughshares, Poetry Daily, Poetry International, Seattle Review, Taos Journal, Tiferet, Traffic East Magazine,* and *Verse Daily*. I'm grateful also to *American Literary Review* and *Ekphrasis* each for awarding me one of their annual poetry prizes.

Thank you especially to several extraordinary, generous, sensitive, and serious readers for comments, suggestions, critiques, and kind words: Ilya Kaminsky and Grace Dane Mazur, especially, and as well to Ira Sadoff, Anne Winters, Marianne Borouch, Lawrence Raab, and also those most splendid of men, warrior poets, the late Thomas Lux, Steve Orlen, and Agha Shahid Ali. Enormous gratitude as well to Anne Rocheleau and to the late Ronni Leopold, each of whom gave me gifts too numerous and varied to mention here except to say they have been spirit guides. For support and inspiration, Carol Ann Davis, Kristina Marie Darling, Marie Gauthier, Veronica Golos, Kirsten Miles, Sarah Russell, Jim Schley, and Dan Beachy-Quick. Fundamental thanks and appreciation to Jessie Lendennie and Salmon Poetry. Finally and most especially, my love to Alexander, my favorite son, and to Cassandra Cleghorn, blessed wife, partner, and spirit guide for her wisdom, kindness, perception, poetic sensibilities, and heart as big as Nebraska.

Photograph: Cassandra Cleghorn

JEFFREY LEVINE is the author of two previous books of poetry: *Rumor of Cortez*, short-listed for the 2006 *Los Angeles Times* Literary Award in Poetry, and *Mortal, Everlasting*, which won the 2002 Transcontinental Poetry Prize. In addition, he is the principal translator from the Spanish of Pablo Neruda's major work, *Canto General*. His many poetry prizes include the Larry Levis Prize from the *Missouri Review*, the James Hearst Poetry Prize from *North American Review*, the *Mississippi Review* Poetry Prize, the *Ekphrasis* Poetry Prize, and the *American Literary Review* poetry prize. His poetry has appeared most recently in *Plowshares*, *Harvard Review*, *Agni*, *Poetry International*, and *Beloit Poetry Journal*, as well as many dozens of other journals and magazines. A graduate of the Warren Wilson MFA Program for Writers, Levine is founder, artistic director and publisher of Tupelo Press, an award-winning independent literary press located in the historic NORAD Mill in the Berkshire Mountains of Western Massachusetts, now in its 20th year of publishing critically important poetry and prose.

salmonpoetry

Cliffs of Moher, County Clare, Ireland

"Like the sea-run Steelhead salmon that thrashes upstream
to its spawning ground, then instead of dying, returns to
the sea – Salmon Poetry Press brings precious cargo to both
Ireland and America in the poetry it publishes, then carries
that select work to its readership against incalculable odds."

TESS GALLAGHER

The Salmon Bookshop
& Literary Centre

Ennistymon, County Clare, Ireland

Listed in *The Irish Times'* 35 Best Independent Bookshops